Second Skin

An anthology of poetry from

The Wirral Young Poets Laureate

~

In memory of Chris Salmon

twf
Publishing

Second Skin

Published in the UK by:
The Writer's Forum Publishing
www.thewritersforum.org.uk

ISBN: 978-0-9564436-3-2

Printed by:
Birkenhead Press
www.birkenheadpress.co.uk

In memory of
Chris Salmon

This anthology is dedicated to the beautiful life of Chris Salmon. There are many things one could say about Chris. He went to Calday Grange Grammar School, where his gentle personality made him popular with pupils and staff alike; he lived at home with his brother Jonny, and his parents, Julie and Rich; he was passionate about English and Russian literature, and wrote his own poetry. Sadly, Chris passed away of a streptococcal infection and pneumonia on the 5th February 2009. He was just fifteen. These days, Chris's memory lives on through his writing: his poetry has been published in conjunction with Calday School in *The Siege of Leningrad,* and is available online at www.chrissalmon.org.uk. The Wirral Young Poets Laureate were honoured to receive his parents' blessing to dedicate this anthology to him.

What do I smell of?

Does this writing stink of me?
Pong of Carol Ann Duffy?
T.S. Elliot, you can't ignore.
Can you smell Marianne Moore?

William Shakespeare,
And Will Wordsworth,
William Blake,
Oh What On Earth?

Clearly seeing Oscar Wilde?
Writing Dahl for my dear child?
Milligan's not your average Joe.
Just like Edgar Allan Poe.

Lewis Carroll, what jabberwocky.
Writing all this fiddly quocky.
Can poetry be more like prose?
A harsh and untamed prickly rose?

Chris Salmon

The Wirral Young Poets Laureate

As Mayor of Wirral, I was delighted to be contacted by Wirral's very first Young Poet Laureate, and Editor of this anthology Holly Green, who asked me if I would write an introductory paragraph for this eagerly anticipated anthology.

The concept of the Young Poet Laureate first saw daylight in 2008, the role being created with a threefold thrust; to raise the profile of young people, poetry, and Wirral.

Holly Green became Wirral's first Young Poet Laureate, cutting through a very tight and articulate pack. The position rapidly took on a great importance to the wider community of Wirral. The fact that so many budding young poets submitted their work for consideration has shown that there is an untapped and exciting seam of expertise in Wirral. It is our job to uncover that expertise, and to help these young poets to hone their skills in the public forum.

The Young Poet Laureate movement is a beacon shining out to young people all over Wirral. Come and see what we are doing! Come and show your poems! Let's see what you can do! Who knows, you could be the next Wirral's Young Poet Laureate!

It is wonderful to know that there are so many gifted and enthusiastic young poets all over Wirral. They are actively dispelling the myths and negativity surrounding "youth culture" in this day and age. Young poets are playing a very valuable part by reaching out to people at so many levels, and not just their own peer groups. These writers are proving that the future of poetry on Wirral is in very safe hands.

Cllr. Alan Jennings
Mayor of Wirral.

Foreword

It has been a real delight to read alongside the Wirral Young Poet Laureates in recent years and to have been invited to become a patron of the project. These young writers impress everyone in their always large audiences with the freshness of their work, their openness and humour, and their considerable performance skills. It's a fantastic idea to offer young poets the opportunity to represent poetry within the community and to develop their own craft in the real, living atmosphere of poetry readings and workshops, in their own schools and libraries. Yes, poets need above all time alone in their garrets; but to be part of the vital relationship between reader and poet, audience and performer, and to discuss poetry with their peers and elders, is quite simply life-changing. I hope the poems here give the reader a glimpse of the sparkling potential which the WYPL scheme has uncovered.

Carol Ann Duffy
Poet Laureate

Holly Green
Wirral's First Young Poet Laureate 2008

As WYPL-in-chief, I wrote and performed poetry for various – and sometimes dubious - private, public and civic events. Since then, I have annoyed audiences at festivals in Chester, Much Wenlock and Wirral BookFest, as well as reading alongside Carol Ann Duffy. I am proud to be one of the Young Laureate Family, and to represent the creativity of Wirral's youth. I dedicate my life to what the WYPLs do best: nicking hats, drinking tea and cracking inappropriate jokes on solemn occasions.

Radio Blues

Softer than April,
Your long hair in the cup,
Your eyes full of something
Azure, barely perceptible,
Woodsmoke almost --
But not quite, wilder.
I remember sitting next to you,
Humming distractions,
The inkstains on my fingers
Showing me up as something unavoidable --
The inevitable garret-crawler,
The ink-fiend.
And yet, hooks,
Little smiling hands
That grasped and pulled,
Pulled irresistibly and –
'Do you like Patti Smith?'
Singing 'Horses' at you,
As though I could sweep us away
With the rhythm and the pulse
And the whole blunt force of the matter --
Chasing us both down rainy streets
In the coldest April we had ever known,
And the giddy fall into bed, 3 am,
Waking at noon with our heads under pillows.
I counted magpies,
As Patti counted horses,
And you laughed and said that the little Gods count birds.
It was superstition,
A vanity, I suppose;
But you understood that the wings

Stood for hope.
New Year, and the frothy explosion,
The misty haloes of breath
That fogged, and refogged,
And came and went with the seasons,
And wishes and fingers,

And hopping for warmth,
Like fleas in a hayrick,
And full of young hope.
That was probably our strength,
When February came,
And I had to let him in,
And the windows rattled with his passing.
And when I stormed, and wept,
And rattled my knuckles,
You told me with discretion
That Patti Smith saw horses, continuously,
And I saw birds.

November 2007: Winning poem, Wirral's Young Poet Laureate 2008

Resurrection

and when you left me,
the sun divorced the sky.
The earth was swallowed
in a plum-soft dark,
as deep and still as snow.
It was winter in my heart --
the brown earth froze
and emptied itself of birds.
I watched them stitch the sky,
their dark wings tearing a symphony of air.
And when the earth warmed
and split beneath my feet,
I knew you would come back.
I watched the sun rise,
spilling her netful of light between the hills -
and on the blue edge of morning,
there you were:
coming back to me through the valley,
the light of morning on your face,
and I knew it was Spring.

April 2008: Easter Assembly, Upton Hall School FCJ

A meeting of the elders

Socrates adjusts his sandals, shuffles parchment, clears his throat.
'Well of course, I see your point Zeus, but there's nothing we can do.'
Zeus sighs and rubs his temples -- far off, rain purples the hilltops.
'If we could just move the bins... *a* bin! Any bin! I just can't stand the
smell, Soc!'
Leonidas scowls at his clotting coffee.
'And that's another thing,' he says, 'Cows. What are they gonna do with
the *cows*
when the new Aldi goes up?'
'The wise man learns from man and beast alike,' lilts Buddha, loosening
his tie.
Tibetan monks feel the weight of revelation touch down massively.
'So I don't see what the problem is. If the badgers dig, they dig! It's a
village green, not flaming Babylon.'
'If we could get back to the agenda,' Socrates offers with futile hope.
'Now the bins -- that, I agree with. But Henry, I don't see your point.'
Martin Luther King declines the biscuits, and turns to Henry the Eighth.
'All I'm saying is, *marriage counselling-*'
'But I think we're missing the point,' squeaks Socrates, the optimist.
'If we could just do something about the-'
'badgers! it's what they do, they-'
'counsel troubled couples! Then we can-'
'Build a new Aldi, innit?'
'QUIET!' Socrates bellows. There is a peace like whales dreaming.
'If we could get back to the *agenda*. Gentlemen, *please*. That's better.
Thank you, that's great. Now then.
The Mayor's coming.
All rise.'

May 2008: the Mayor-Making ceremony

11

The Secret Garden

In number nine, there is the man from a Polish town:
before the day picks up her comb
and shakes out her bright hair,
he breathes the quiet air
and sings in his mother tongue.

Number eleven hears the lilt and stall of his Polish song
and takes it with her.
As the morning gathers speed,
she warms her cocoa on the stove's blue tongue
and says a prayer:
for parking spaces,
sunshine, half-price gas
and a plague on taxmen.

Number twelve will say a different prayer --
all day, she counts in the gathering light
the miracles she needs for the child inside her:
big skies, lollipop men,
guardian angels
and the life well lived.

God has no business creating in Number four --
theirs is a house of finished things,
where the afternoon lies around in polished lozenges.
The ladies of the house are sweet as frosted teacakes,
at eighty-four, barely even fifteen:
They still gossip in whispers,
as if every surface in the house had ears.

They share their secrecy with Number twenty-seven:
the girl there has her best friend round
like a part-time Siamese twin.
Their cigarette smoke signals on the air behind the tool shed,
as they curse and giggle like junior witches.

Everyone here is each other's best-kept secret,
no more than curtain patterns, peeling paint and aspidistras.
They are slices of wall that lighten in sunlight,
parked cars, a song in the morning,
before the milkman.
The evening fades and goes out,
quietly.

May 2008: Oxton Secret Gardens

Anthem for Doomed Youth

What passing-bells for these who die as cattle?
Only a hillside's shoal of homely lights,
a skein of scars,
a sleeping woman's hair.
No mockeries for them; no prayers nor bells;
nor any voice of mourning save the birds'--
a blackbird's diamond song in morning sky,
before the scarlet flowers touch the air.
What candles may be held to speed them all?
Only their listed names and dying hours,
not in the hands of boys, but in their hearts.
What passing-bells for these who die as cattle?
Only the blue-sky faces of the young,
a scarlet flower, a country's untouched earth,
and each slow dusk, a drawing down of blinds.

November 2008: Remembrance Sunday

Icarus

Your wings are frail,
webs of skin between
sickly fingers of bone.
The sun's fierce kiss could
earth you like a volt.
There is a fire in you,
a knotted cramp of lust
like your own religion.
You wear the crash mats thin,
wear bruises like a tropical disease,
wear out your mother's patience
with trials of home-made flight.
Sometimes,
it feels like you will not succeed.
I know the sky is yours:
it hangs all day,
a gasp of burning blue,
and waits for you.
It knows you'll grow your bones,
two wings
like a sudden shock of icicles,
like a stripe of fire.
It knows
you've got a magpie's heart.

November 2008: for the inauguration of Wirral's Young Poet Laureate 2009

On Loss

The things we learned at school,
in faded classrooms dimmed by time
that settles on our days
like so much dust --

so often, these are what we call to mind
when Change yanks up the fabric of our lives
and shakes out all good sense
and leaves us dazed:

so, when his child is sick,
a pacing man may lift his voice
and chant the nine times table
like a prayer;

or, when her heartbeat,
for a second, drops its tune,
an anxious woman's tongue is loosed
in spelling out the names of Spanish towns.

Then, dear one, let me soothe your heart with this:
energy, they say, is never lost,
but only trades its form for something new:

so may my sleeping breath,
when I am gone, be brought back
as a blazing tiger's roar;
so, likewise, may my voice
become the song
that brims from every morning blackbird's throat;

and so, love,
may my heart become a seed --

life's tiny, stubborn core,
that holds within its slender self
the promise of a tree.

For, though they didn't teach us this at school,
these truths are what we've sifted for ourselves:
that this is how the world rewrites itself;
that loss is only energy that's changed.

March 2010: for the memorial service of Elizabeth Doran (née Hughes)

Lizz Clark
Wirral's Young Poet Laureate 2009

During my 'reign' as Young Poet Laureate, I read poetry with lunatics. The Scaffold, feminists and Carol Ann Duffy. I read at a Remembrance Day service and in strangers' gardens. I went to Shropshire and back on a coach full of Wirral Poets, and stole a straw hat ...
... Je ne regrette rien.

Individuals

When we wore wasted Converse we were wanted.

We drew on our hands, shared winegums,
pierced, plucked, dyed,
rebelled, resisted, jumped or didn't,
followed, tried to start something.

We failed. (Sometimes on purpose.)

In the mewling of the mob we heard our
voices from without ourselves.
We liked it.

We knew what we wanted. (Possibly.)
We knew what was best for ourselves, every time.
We knew everything. We could fly.

We could fall, too. We found that
out later. In the wilderness of life
we were a pack, a pride. Before the fall.

November 2008: Winning poem, Wirral's Young Poet Laureate 2009

Mayor-making

Are you ready? Are you good with
games, with words -- quick on your feet and the uptake as well?
Put it like this: can you stand to stand
at a civic event, huddled damp in a circle of brolleyed dry land,
pretend it's not pouring and shake my hand
(all the while grinning like everything's grand)?

Can you make good impressions, make all the right noises?
Stand up for yourself? For me? For us all?
Can you live up to legacies, what's gone before?
Will you know when to step up and
when to back down?

Is the feel of this place in your bones? On your skin?
Do you wear the air like a hat; the streaky grey sky as a scarf,
a belt? Do you know our inside jokes, our tics? The way we
breathe in glorious history and breathe out life,
community? Do you?

To coin a phrase: this land's the place I love.
Others can come and go, but here and now watch me throw
down the gauntlet: you must hold. Hold fast.

May 2009: the Mayor-Making ceremony

Roses

You like the roses. Or do they like you?

The period details on the costume of the garden
they are timeless. You are now
(so hard it hurts), but sometimes,
out there, for some people,
anything can be at any time
and you are no exception. You fit in.
Viewed from beyond the hedge, your pure
uniqueness looks at once at home among the roses,
harmonises, matches, slides right in, makes sense.

It is a dance.
They open up their curling Fibonacci heads as you pass by:
they nod, and you nod back. And it begins.
The crowd of circling colours shifts in draughts
stirred by your hands and arms,
the outer layers you discard.

I see you dancing
past the window of my study, lift my head from books
to watch you twirl over the lawn.

It is unfair.

May 2009: Oxton Secret Gardens

The Eldest

Red curtains ripple outwards and the air is thick
as greasepaint. Please arrange yourselves
precisely, girls, unfurl your curls and twirl your skirts
in neat and even drapes. You must be perfect.

She remembers -- it was years ago --
the country boy who bought her pony when she grew
too old to ride it; his deft fingers and his easy laugh,
the way he hunkered down without a thought to greet

the little thing, so weak and small compared to him.
The painter calls her 'madam'. In the thousand times
she moves her head and makes the light all wrong,
he does not touch her. She can feel

his work-flushed heat across the inch of space
between his fingers and her face.
Like this, madam. No, no, like this.
He sits her in a tableau'd fakery and tells her

to enjoy herself: she pours the tea and lets it
taste the air for half a second,
then fall down and in, contained again.

October 2009: National Poetry Day reading at the Williamson Art Gallery,
Birkenhead

Poetry

It is not as if it matters
in the sword-and-sandals, cheese-and-pickle scheme of things

that ink-stained fingers on some stranger's hand
moved, years and lifetimes back,
in that strange dance we take for granted now,
and wrote. A word. Another.

That is not the point.
It is the building of a card-house, but it's not
the act of holding things just right (precision, patience)
that impresses: no. If you could
build the Taj Mahal of water, not of stone,
or catch the smell of tarmac in a fish-net, or
weave clothes from sand and seaweed strands --

if you could set alight the paper passions
of the long-dead dramatists,
undo the buttons of the pompous laureates,
unearth the chains that bind, shackle, divide us,
help to find a key --

that would be good. That would be poetry.

October 2009: National Poetry Day

11/11

I'm sure they cut your letters up
and put them
        back together
                differently. They read
like someone else's lines, the workings of your
phrases mutilated
mangled as by shrapnel wounds
disjointed, wrong –
you met me at the station like a silent ghost;
in uniform you were a stranger, shaven-headed, unsmiling

I saw you as at 16, Harlequin,
all brightly coloured
        missing cues and laughing
        corpsing, you told me,
        that's what the actors call it

My Pinocchio,
                You learned to tie yourself
to unseen forces up above
before you tied your own shoelaces –
basic training drilled in

with the ABC, the poetry and heraldry
and song (yes sir, it starts early –)

Remember how I held your hand
in church, the day before you left,
and prayed or hoped –?
But love, like loss, is blunt – cannot cut strings.

November 2009: Remembrance Sunday

24

What You're Letting Yourself In For

(And maybe there are no winged sandals. No-one
floats to earth on fluffy white marshmallow clouds
and says, trust me, you will do well. And by the way
watch out for –)

If they wrote down enough numbers
they could map the future out in marker-pen,
they say, in ink -- indelible. But if I held

the book of prophecies, the auguries,
the findings of the number-crunching oracle,
the printout from the prophecy machine,

I'd have to burn it. (I would rather live as unforeseen
as pirates, as non-sequitur
                    ... as poetry.)

November 2009: for the inauguration of Wirral's Young Poet Laureate 2010

Maria Stebbing
Wirral's Deputy Young Poet Laureate 2009

Being a part of the Wirral Young Poet Laureates has been an invaluable experience. I have revelled in all of the events, bonded with other writers, developed a more professional attitude to writing, and hold a greater appreciation of other writers' work. I am reading English & Creative Writing at John Moore's University, hoping to be a writer and to encourage budding writers to persevere with such a prolific and accessible gift.

Touch Is A Silent Language

Touch is a silent language,
It yells as our lips meet, and
Whispers as we embrace.

Love is like the thrash of waves against
Our land.
Powerful, delicate.
Beautiful.

The realisation of love is like a sudden
Gulp of air in our lungs.
Unnerving. Life.

Our hearts pound and fill with joy and content
By the mere thought of them,
Their simple presence in our life like
A hurricane in our mundane routine.

Their laugh and smile are conquering,
Making us laugh too,
Even if we are sad, angry, or hurt.

It is giddiness, breathlessness,
Excitement.
All mingled into one explosive
Enlightenment.

They are like the sun in our sky,
And moon of our night.
Making us sing and
Dance and giggle with all our might.

Pinks and reds and maroons,
Entwined with teddy-bears, Valentine's
Cards, roses!
All make sense now.

Touch is like a silent language,
An unbreakable bond far more
Than just skin deep.
It is love.

November 2008: Winning poem, Wirral's Deputy Young Poet Laureate
2009

Dawn Fantasies

I want to walk through dawn
with you.

Hear the birds that chirp for you;
Touch the zephyr that glides for you;
Feel the grass that quivers for you.
Sense my heart that beats for you.

And as our souls meet,
and the sun does eventually shine
- the world was glorious already to us -
our meeting, our morning,
our lifetime,
is divine.

Music to our ears, and
ecstasy to our eyes.

The joys of nature!

Love to our hearts.

May 2009: Oxton Secret Gardens

Unclaimed

Twisted, entangled,
Broken spectacle frames.
Unclaimed.

A mountain of shoes
Which have treaded through summer, snow, wind, and rain.
Unclaimed.

Tumbling locks of women,
Who once possessed proud, flowing manes.
Unclaimed.

Tiny garments of children who were not aware
Of the finality that they faced on the trains.
Unclaimed.

The paintings, poems, inventions, cures,
Music, awards, deserved fame.
Unclaimed.

The photographs, the memories,
All of joy, love, and promise -- no pain.
Unclaimed.

The addressed suitcases, the individual, precious belongings,
The hopes, the dreams, all planned and pre-ordained.
Unclaimed.

The experiences, the future, the legacies;
The continuation of family idiosyncrasies and names.
Unclaimed.

The children, grandchildren, descendants.

Individuality, culture, neighbourhoods, lives, which never came.
All unclaimed.

October 2009: Wirral BookFest

Love is Simple

Love is simple.

It shouldn't be difficult,
Make believe,
Force-yourself-to-think-they're-the-one.

No.
Just simple.

It is easy; it just happens.

It is the sudden realisation that you are complete.

They <u>are</u> the other half of your coin.

They love you conditionally,
And you love your 'one' unconditionally.

It is innocent, joyful, beautiful.
All-consuming.

It is
I-can't-forget-this-feeling.
It is
I-can't-ignore-this-love.

It follows you all day,
It is with you all day, like your own beating heart.

April 2010: Much Wenlock Poetry Festival

Valentine Part II

Not a red heart or satin rose.

I give you an orange.
It is a sun adorned in luminous paper.
It promises beauty,
Like the intricate unfolding of love.

Here.
It will blind you with sweetness,
Like a lover.
It will make your reflection
A static photo of serenity.

I am trying to be fanciful.
Not a kissogram or cute card.

I give you an orange.
Its tangy kiss will stay on your lips,
Patient and fervent
As we are,
For as long as we are.

Take it.
Its webbed segments will shrink to a smile,
If you like.
Beautiful.
Its scent will cling to your fingers,
Cling to your lips.

April 2010: Much Wenlock Poetry Festival

WYPL: Poetical Progression

Poetry.
A hidden song,
Waiting to burst out.

A secret blend of vocabulary,
Intended for the rhetorical,
Like the seeds and water for a beautiful flower.

A pen.
The wand of the writer,
Conjuring magical literature.

A notebook.
Scribbled, smudged, erased verses
Made, initially, for one ear.

An audience,
Attentively imagining the language of a poet's soul.

An anthology.
The printed, bold, underlined success of your poetical genius.

The Wirral Young Poet Laureate:
Supportive, creative alliances; momentous events;
Unforgettable memories.

An embarkation;
A way in.

November 2009: for the inauguration of Wirral's Young Poet Laureate 2010

Jess Yung
Wirral's Young Poet Laureate 2010

Hello, everybody. I am a pupil at Birkenhead High School, studying Biology, Chemistry, Mathematics and English Literature. I love to read, write, listen to music, draw and dance - albeit not very well, but I do. Reaching the dizzy heights of Young Poet Laureate has opened up new world of literary wonders: reading poetry in Oxton Secret Gardens and Much Wenlock, writing commissions and making great poetry friends.

Remembrance

Like...
Black tears, Silver spots.
Sea of the sky, Grey as it cries.
Vermillion hues, Emerald hands
Spanning upwards as they clasp together.
Forgotten blues, Remembered yellows,
Splintered doors, empty as they stare.

Like...
Tea-stained maps, Jet-scarred carpets
Burned like a sigh breathed in winter.
Birds of Paradise, Apple trees
Blossomed in Heaven's Light.
The Aureole crows and the Poppy seeds
Feeding on the blood of many.

We entered that room together
With beating eyes and tearful hearts.
Ah, Memory, like a sin.
Our waning spirits, our fraying minds
Shattered like a shell as you reach for me.

November 2010: Winning poem, Wirral's Young Poet Laureate 2010

Crimson Winter

Snowfall, winter's bliss,
Icy breezes, a gentle kiss.

Branches wave in the crystal white clouds.
Leaves have fallen, littering the ground.
Grey blue sunlight scattered like seeds
Sowing the grass with silver tears.

Day by day that second skin grows.
Winter's frosty fingers: perverse, relentless.
Children's hands clothed in woollen gloves
Softened by their mother's soothing kiss.

Clasped hands, huddled hearts that meet,
Like kindred spirits embraced in the sleet.

Gaping hearts, warmed by candles,
Red green shimmers cascading downs the walls.
White lights dim in foggy streets
Like stars fallen from the Heavens.

As rain becomes snow,
A million eyes watch in wonder,
At last in unison, acting as one
Mind, body, soul, intertwined by winter's gift.

With new hopes and forgotten memories,
Black with regret and distant reveries.

Unheard cries shattered and broken,
Words that were left ignored, unspoken,
Permeating through the jovial mist.
The empty chair stares back.

The unseen touch, the unheard laughter,
We'll remember when we see that proud flag fly
Our dreams will melt into spring
Like the crimson snow that falls.

December 2010: Birkenhead High School's Christmas Concert

School Time Revelations

Have you ever wondered
What lies beyond that silver rainbow?
Beyond the horizon of white haze
Beyond the shadows of purple winds
Beyond the unchanging blue sky
Waiting...
Like a tigress
Enshrined in tangerine silk
Surrounded by golden scars
Natural...
Godly...
Alive...
Well...?
Have you ever wondered
What lies beyond that mass of cloud?
Beyond your fingertips
As you reach, reach, reach...
And stop.
Hand suspended
Like your heart
Waiting...
For that pinnacle moment
Just there...

You clasp your hand
And realise...

The teacher's just asked you a question.

April 2010: Much Wenlock Poetry Festival

For The Wirral: Our Home

The Wirral is indefinable.
The Wirral wears many clothes.
It comes in all shapes and sizes,
All Colours and Faiths.
Its face changes like the seasons.
Its voice takes on many forms:
Old and Young; Male and Female.
The Wirral is a Rare Kind,
So small the world cannot see it,
So large its inhabitants never tire of it,
 So special that time itself does not change it...
But one hand can,
One voice can,
One leader can change its fate:
Our Mayor,
In whom we trust.
So take the torch and
Write your name on the pages of history.
Take the reins and
Carve our future.
For tomorrow is another day
In our home,
The Wirral,
Our Wirral.

May 2010: Mayor-Making ceremony

Poetry: Secret Garden

Vast emerald shards erupt
From currents of lush brown
Waving with white shoots
Lead by the soft green of new life.
Buds that shy away,
Petals that dust the wind
Like misinformed snow,
Leaves that shudder in the breezes,
Clapping a gentle rhythm as the orchestra plays,
Singing soft tunes you will
Know, Remember and Treasure,
Memories, Dreams and Fantasies will flower,
While Secrets, like seeds, are sown into the soul
Blossoming in the hidden glade.
Undisturbed, Untouched, Unseen.
Crystals of dewfall come to rest here,
Kissing the skin with a ghostly touch
Cooling, Soothing, Haunting,
Lingering as you look on.

Once more...

Once more

Splitting, germinating, rising,

As Spring Returns.

With arms spread and eyes closed
The softest touch to the fingertips
The sweetest scents of
Colours that seep into your world.

Our world.
Our Secret Garden.

May 2010: Oxton Secret Gardens

For The Wirral: Our People

The Wirral is indefinable.
It wears many clothes.
Comes in all shapes and sizes-
In all Colours and Faiths.
Its face changes like the seasons.
So small the world cannot see it,
So large its inhabitants never tire of it,
So special that time itself does not change it.
All but the people.
Life visits.
Life leaves.
Your footprints will be forever behind you.
You've carved your own history with
A name,
A face,
A faith,
A race,
A gender.
You've written your story on the pages of sand and
Watched patiently as it sifts through the generations to come.
Take the reins and
Never regret the past,
Never wander in the present,
Never lose faith in the future,
For tomorrow is another day
For our people,
The people of the Wirral,
Our Wirral.

October 2010: Chris Salmon Poetry Extravaganza Launch Night

Special Illusion

I'm a top magician.

Although you remain ignorant to the
Truth behind the brilliance of a beautiful story,
Painted with the most skilled mind and
Crafted by the brightest hand,
Listen.
See.
Man is a book.
Beginning to end.
The cover as crimson as an execution,
The spine as hard as bone.
The pages as crisp as fresh snow.
The ink as black as your inner eye.

The jet-scarred hands sweep across the
Disconsolate marble face of the Grandfather clock,
Its Golden pendulum swinging
To and fro
To and fro
To and...

You won't hear.
You won't see.
Man is a book.
Beginning to end.

My writing like drunken spiders of tar
Dancing across the tome with
Distinct resolution.
I'll spin my web,
Entice you,
Enchant you,

Drawing you in.
Yes.
I am a top magician.

October 2010: Wirral BookFest

Promise of Remembrance

Tell me, Dear One, as I stand on the edge
With my heart in my hands.
The earth is barren but for the crimson jewels
You had planted in your soul.
For whom do these bells toll?

I'll reap the saddened pride when I see those beauties,
Bounteous as they bow in the wind,
That sharp, whistling wind...
Dear One, did it sound like this then?
Buried in the depths of No Man's Land.

Tell me, Dear One, is this rain the
Thousands of Tears that you shed alone?
The Tears I never saw?
The Tears they never knew?
Some say, "Rain is the Weeping of Angels."

Are you an angel now, Dear One?
Watching as I,
Though atheists pray little,
Offer my words of Peace?
Recounting my Promises against Yours.

Tell me, Dear One, if I call your name,
Do you hear it in this desperate silence?
Call mine. I'll listen.
Though Terror deafens my ears,
Is it your voice in these hollow winds?

Precious few things in this physical world, Dear One,
Grace existence with a glimmer of Hope.
Pandora's Box of the Earth's Core.
Memories: jet-scarred, singed, battered and broken,
One by one, I will count on my fingers.

Dear One:

For every one memory in Pain you spent,
A vow to Peace I shall invent.
For every one moment in shattered Madness,
Two minutes Silence I shall spend in Sadness.
For every one Crimson Flower worn,
A White Blossom I shall adorn.

"We Will Remember Them" wholeheartedly, indeed.
Remember, too, my Vows, Dear One.
For Peace, For Freedom, For Another Tomorrow.

November 2010: Remembrance Sunday

Hannah Kelly
Wirral's Deputy Young Poet Laureate 2010

I'm Hannah, an overgrown toddler/gran hybrid, who spends most of the time drinking weak tea, and watching Australian soaps with my cats. My lifetime to-do list includes to be able to do a cartwheel without falling on my bum; keep a tomato plant alive long enough to harvest it; and to somehow make a living from baking nice cakes and spending a lot of time asleep. Being a part of the yuh-wipples (sorry, Young Wirral Poet Laureates) has introduced me into a strange but brilliant world. I'm very glad it did so before I made my university course choices, as I'm not sure I would make a very good orthoptist.

Ode to Oxygen

Each of my allotropes
Understand your every molecule.
Though if we're talking nanochemistry, I guess that won't impress you.

You've delocalised all of my electrons
Each tender touch forms another covalent bond
I long for you
In my lonely salt solution.

I've been getting the current from Anode and Cathode
They tell me to make th-th-th-the first move
I'm worried
That my atoms aren't massive enough to get you to like me
How many half-lives must I decay through?
All I want is to change state in your eyes.

Bond with me baby, we can make things happen.
I've never doubted that we're a match made in conical flask.

Come 'ed darlin', everyone knows.

Everyone knows that we can make holes in the atmosphere.

I've been getting the current from Anode and Cathode
They tell me to make th-th-th-the first move
I'm worried
That my atoms aren't massive enough to get you to like me
How many half-lives must I decay through?
All I want is to change state in your eyes.

I'll be anything you want, any state any allotrope
Anything you want, any state any allotrope.
Diamond? Graphite?
Buckminster fullerene, I'm all yours.

November 2009: Winning poem, Wirral Deputy Young Poet Laureate 2010

Renie's Dress

She makes it for her wedding day
Clean, crisp and white.
In the pictures with her new husband
Neat rows of covered buttons,
The zip that doesn't quite match.
Later, she dyes it black, for a second use:
An unrivalled evening gown
Lifts and shivers when she moves
Flows silently liquid to the floor when still.

I stand in the dress.
Younger than she was by a year or two
And, although I can safely say that I'm no fatty,
The bodice struggles to contain my ribcage
The tired zip almost wheezing.
We found her precious ring in a green satin box,
It just wiggles onto my ring finger, a perfect fit.

This woman died in ninety-four
And I now inherit her
Knitting needles, buttons, real tweed, fake fur, almost velvet.
She was gone, before I had the chance
To find out more
Hear her stories
Learn her wisdoms

February 2009

Carni-Bores

For reasons I cannot remember
I attended a party last November.
The host of which had gone "all out"
On beef and pork and fowl and trout
All laboriously prepared in modern ways
(The guests could not avert the gaze)

I nudged my neighbour, but before my question,
He shook his head, and mumbled a mention
"As a famous man once said,
There was a thing, but now... it's dead?"

He sighed and our hostess piped in
Blue eyes quite bright, but dark with gin --
"I shan't further contemplate these visions
Until we've had some more provisions,
And unless I'm very much mistaken
Everyone would like more bacon!"

If I'd stayed later (for I left quite early)
I would have surely contracted scurvy.

April 2010: Much Wenlock Poetry Festival

Gazing Into Infinity For Amateurs

I recently rediscovered a trick from my childhood;
If you close your eyes,
Press your sockets with your thumbs
And concentrate on seeing, not being shown,
You see what infinity looks like

Or, at least, what I think it looks like
(Lots of dull, faraway lights that are difficult to focus on,
If you're interested)

It comforts me that infinity can fit between my thumb and eye pit
Makes you realise that no matter how big anything is,
You can close your eyes and pretend it's an inch-and-a-half wide.

Afterwards, I feel quite daft
When I open my eyes and find I've lost a contact lens.
Maybe next time I'll just read a book or something,
And save myself the apologetic trip to Boots.

June 2010: Birkenhead Sixth Form College poetry competition – 'Space'

Little Man

Little man,
Let your sister play,
And try not to let her fall.
Try to realise that you annoy
with your squeals of "my ball!"

Little man,
When you realise your parents
Aren't masters of the universe,
Be respectful and contextual,
Don't assume you'll get there first.

Little man,
It is far from weak
to show your true position.
Being outright and clear with those you love
Reaps a soul's nutrition.

Little man,
When you're older and
You get to have your say,
Don't abuse it or confuse it with
Another chance to get your way.

Little man,
When your little man
Sits on your aged knee
Tell him all you can about the world,

And give him love from me.

July 2010

The Poet Who Isn't Quite Sure If She Knows It Or Not

For me, poetry... Well I never was fond
They were boring and long
About springtime or wartime
A big weighty chore of mine
Reeking gee-cee-ess-ees
And "interpret-as-you-please"
Well, excuse me.

I'm a child of my generation
Suckled on teletubbies and CGI animation
Used to instant gratification.
Of course I read grown-up books
(Mainly just so I can throw judgemental looks)
I've found my cosy social nook.

But, one day, on a whim
I found myself let in
With a Waterstone's token
And my poetic silence broken.
Ok, so I'm clearly no 'pro'
(As you're sure to now know)
My attempts at iambic pentameter
Are about as convincingly regular
As the bus I get to school
With my rhyming style 'typically un-cool'.

But I've got my 'young' title for a reason
So I can get up to my knees in
Finding my feet
(If you'll pardon the pun.
I'm sure I'll grow out of finding them fun)

So, in twenty years time
Come back and you'll find
A starving artiste
Who solely can feast
On her bitterly critical

Observations political...
More likely, perhaps
I'll just have lots of cats

With no one to read the works of my Bic
(Undoubtedly formed into limerick)
And every night I'll fret
That no one's made my Wikipedia entry yet.

October 2010: Wirral BookFest

Backword

In 2007, I was fed up reading in the Press about dissolute, disaffected, dissipated youth. If we were to accept the common misconception of how young people misspent the golden asset of youth, then those of us who survived would climb the nearest Jacob's Ladder to the moon and take shelter in the Sea of Tranquility.

And yet, all the young people I meet are as far from that misperceived concept as the moon. The answer was simple. Raise the profile of all the young people who have a positive, productive, creative outlook on life and their futures.

The first step was to tap into the rich seam of creativity which exists in the 'next' generation. Having always had a leaning to writing and the use of language, it occurred to me that we should find the means to give young people a feeling of status, and thus the Wirral Young Poet Laureate was born.

The Laureate, an 'official' Wirral Council post, represents the Borough in civic, public and private events, and is commissioned to write and read a poem for the inauguration of the Mayor, the Remembrance Parade, Oxton Secret Gardens, Folk on the Coast Festival, Much Wenlock Poetry Festival and several others.

As that first day of poetical judgment approached, I waited worryingly for Jo Bell, Cheshire Poet Laureate, to pronounce her choice; my confidence wavered between ending up with somebody who couldn't spell and a future best-seller.

I 'misgived' in vain. The first Wirral Young Poet Laureate, Holly Green, Upton Hall School, more than fulfilled my expectations. And the WYPL 2009, Liz Clark, and her deputy, Marie Stebbings, both proved to be more than worthy of their posts. And the current Laureate, Jessica Yung, and her Deputy, Hannah Kelly, sustain that poetical standard.

The choosing of the 2011/12 Laureate will be through the Chris

Salmon Foundation, which is sponsoring an annual Poetry Competition, which, as well as awarding prizes for three categories of poets, will select the overall winner as the next Wirral Young Poet Laureate.

And when I sent some samples of the young poets work to Carol Ann Duffy, the English Poet Laureate, and invited her to be the patron, there was no hesitation.

It bursts my heart with pride to read the poems in this anthology.

John Gorman

Index of Poem Titles